Claus-Jürgen Höper · Ulrike Kutzleb
Alke Stobbe · Bertram Weber

Translated by Hilary Davies

AWARENESS GAMES
Personal Growth through Group Interaction

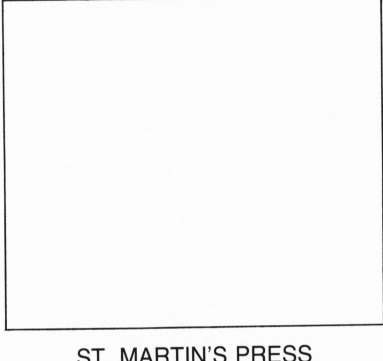

ST. MARTIN'S PRESS
New York

Originally published in Germany under the title
Die Spielende Gruppe Copyright © 1974 by
Jugenddienst-Verlag, Wuppertal
Translation Copyright © 1975 by St. Martin's Press, Inc.
For information, write:
St. Martin's Press
175 Fifth Avenue
New York, N.Y. 10010
Manufactured in the United States of America
Designed by Robert Carola after the German edition
Library of Congress Catalog Card Number: 75-37964

Published simultaneously in U. K. by St. James Press
For information, write:
St. James Press Ltd.
3 Percy Street
London W1P 9FA

Library of Congress Cataloging in Publication Data

Main entry under title:
Awareness games

Translation of Die spielende Gruppe
Bibliography: p.
1. Group relations training. 2. Group games.
I. Höper, Claus-Jürgen.
HM134.s6913 1976   158'.1   75-37964

ISBN-06265-6-Casebound
ISBN-06300-8-Paperback

Contents

AWARENESS GAMES

Introduction

Anyone concerned with group dynamics, particularly anyone who wants to put theory into practice, may wonder where to get directions or suggestions for "group dynamics games." For this collection we have devised some new games and compiled and modified some existing ones. The games create areas within which human behavior can be experienced in play form. They enable members of a group
—to get to know their own behavior and its effect on others;
—to experience various forms of communication consciously;
—to express emotions and react appropriately to the emotions of others;
—to be confronted with conflicts and decisions;
—to observe, recognize, and change roles and fixed behavior patterns in themselves; and
—to experience and reject control and authority.

The effectiveness of the games depends largely on the competence of the game leader; this collection is intended primarily for students of group dynamics and educators who have not only theoretical knowledge but also sufficient experience of group games to determine the suitability of particular games and foresee their consequences. The game leader must also understand his own function in directing the games. Interest and good intentions are not enough. The games we present offer the opportunity for emotional and social learning. In our selection we have favored games that create model situations where behavior patterns can be consciously perceived. These patterns can be discussed in the group and possibly altered. A discussion may also give rise to new responses which can be explored in a model situation, a game situation, without fear of possible consequences. A game without subsequent discussion therefore seems pointless; discussion is an integral part of the game and calls for the participation of people not involved in the game.

Games also offer the opportunity of setting group processes in motion, making the players aware of them and of how they may be used in the future.

This collection should not be regarded as a series of ready-made instructions—"a suitable game for every situation"—to be carried out systematically (or even in the given order.) Instead, we hope it will stimulate readers to adapt the games to suit their situation and improvise using their own ideas, and that readers will let us have reports of their experiences in putting it into practice.

And let's not forget that it's in the nature of games to afford fun and pleasure!

Hamburg, June 1974

Claus-Jürgen Höper
Ulrike Kutzleb
Alke Stobbe
Bertram Weber

Key to Game Descriptions

Duration: Basically, the time given is meant only as a rough guide. It is intended, first, to give you an approximate idea of how long the game will last, and second (and more important), to help answer the question: Is the game dragging on too long, or is the group "tearing through it"? The length of a game also depends on the size of the group; the suggested time refers to a group of the size recommended.

The duration of a game is often so dependent on the composition of the group and the situation that it is impossible for us to give an estimated time. With many games the best rule is: "Only play as long as it's fun."

Age group: This figure should also be regarded only as a guide. Upper and lower limits depend on the composition of the group itself.

Size of group: The number of participants should not vary significantly from the number given. If the group is too large the game leader and any observers will not be able to keep track of the game, and not everyone will be able to take part in the ensuing discussion. Games played in a group that is too large produce too many random impressions, and in too small a group they may become monotonous because of a lack of stimulus.

Materials: Paper, pens, scissors, etc. that are needed for each game are listed so that they may be assembled before the game is begun and do not cause interruptions later.

Learning goal: We have given the particular learning goal of a game only when it is not already apparent from the title, the chapter introduction, or description of the game.

Game sequence: A step-by-step description of the game.

What to watch out for: We have only included criteria that are essential for the game in question, not general ones.

Discussion aids: This category indicates problems that may arise during the game that ought to be discussed, as well as questions that may be touched on in the game which can be talked over independently. It is often wise to play the game again after the discussion, in order to try out new behavior patterns.

Warning: Some games are not universally applicable. The chapter introductions indicate general difficulties; this category points to the special dangers to watch out for in each game. It's better to leave out a game rather than take an incalculable risk.

I. Introducing Yourself and Getting Acquainted

Introducing Yourself and Getting Acquainted

We have given the introductory phase special treatment since it has a particular significance for group dynamics. Chapters 2–5 (Communication and Group Formation, Observation and Perception, Identification and Empathy, Aggression and Self-Assertion) may be taken in any order, but introducing yourself and getting acquainted must come first. In the introductory phase players reveal more than just their names; the pattern of each individual's attitude, behavior, and role function within the group is also determined. Since this phase requires considerable emotional involvement (in some cases it may cause identity crises) the individual's attitude here can be decisive for her or his later position in the group. Behavior patterns that crystallize during this phase prefigure future behavior. And this is precisely the function of the introduction games: they not only set the group process in motion, but also make the individual player consider and express her or his expectations, misgivings, and preconceptions in relation to herself or himself and to the group. These games reveal the group's tendencies in the game situation, and point the way toward possible learning goals for subsequent games. In other words the introduction phase should be understood and used as more than just an isolated step at the beginning of the group process.

The *goals* of the various introduction games are manifold: to bring about initial contact between group members, to break down shyness and inhibitions, and to help to overcome fears, such as the fear of talking in public.

Since the roles of individual "players" are of equal importance and interchangeable, this equality influences the overall situation of each of the players: prejudices are more easily broken down, the formation of cliques is prevented; existing outsiders can more easily step out of role; and potential outsiders can integrate more readily into the group.

Game playing that is not obviously goal-directed has its own value and should be tolerated from the start. It encourages spontaneity and more creative group work. The relative vagueness of certain games' objectives allows participants to assess the situation for themselves, to sound out the atmosphere—"How are the others behaving?" "Are people showing their feelings or concealing them?" This initial assessment of the group not only helps the individual sympathize with others, but also makes each person examine her- or himself. Group members are encouraged not only to become conscious of their own impressions, feelings, wishes, and expectations in relation to the group but also to express them and possibly put them into practice. This can result in the emancipation of the individual in relation to the group, as well as the emancipation of the group as a whole in relation to the group leader.

In choosing games you should consider the following: Do members of the group know each other already? Is the group accustomed to game-playing or not? Are they children, teenagers, or adults? These conditions will largely determine whether the participants in your group find it more or less difficult to do or say something they are not used to, to speak to someone they don't know, or to talk in front of a large group of people.

You should also keep in mind in the beginning that it is generally unwise to have group discussion on the behavior of individuals during games. Such discussion is only constructive when a mutual trust has developed between members, so that observations can be properly understood, considered, and discussed.

1 Introducing Yourself and Getting Acquainted
Hiding names and finding them

Duration:	about 15 minutes
Age group:	children and teenagers
Size of group:	8–20
Materials:	finger paints, felt pens, paper, cardboard, glue or transparent tape, safety pins, etc.

Players conceal their names on themselves in such a way that anyone who wishes to read them has to make direct contact. For instance: write your name on your arm in washable finger paint and pull your sleeve down over it; stick your name onto your belt buckle; write your name in mirror writing; write your name on a piece of paper and hang it around your neck.

Age group: all ages

Materials: paper, different colored felt pens

Participants introduce themselves to the group one by one, by writing their names and drawing a picture of themselves on a piece of paper on the wall.

There *may* be discussion afterward (in pairs or in the group) about people's feelings and observations about introducing themselves.

What to watch out for:

What is people's handwriting like—disjointed, angular, rhythmic, large or small?
Which colors do they use?

Warning:

It's generally unwise to collect and analyze with the group observations on individuals' behavior immediately after this game. Being "challenged" too soon often intimidates members of the group so badly that it's impossible to continue working with them.

3 Introducing Yourself and Getting Acquainted
The seat on my right is free

Duration: as long as everyone is enjoying it; not too long

Age group: children and teenagers

Size of group: 8–20

All players sit in a circle. One seat remains empty. The player to the left of the empty seat begins:
   "The seat on my right is free,
   I want [Sally] next to me."
The game should be played at a brisk pace.

Warning:

It's important that everyone be involved in the game, so it is wise for the game leader to help direct the proceedings.

Duration: about 15 minutes

Age group: all ages

Size of group: depends on the probable memorizing talents of participants

The players sit in a circle. One says her or his name; the neighbor on the left repeats the name and adds her or his own. Then the neighbor on the left continues. Each player repeats all the names that have been said so far and finally adds her or his own. The game goes on until everyone has had a turn. If the group is very large, players may repeat only the last four names.

Warning:

Since this game calls for purely cognitive memory skill, it may cause embarrassment to some individuals.

5 Introducing Yourself and Getting Acquainted
Name and gesture

Age group: all ages

Size of group: optional

Everyone stands in a circle. One by one the players say their names and make some gesture or movement. The whole group repeats the name and the movement.

What to watch out for:

Which players make gestures by themselves?
Which ones use partners?
How much space do they take up in making their gestures?
Who breaks the rules of the game by commenting on her or his own gesture?

Warning:

Adults and very inhibited groups may be intimidated by having to express themselves nonverbally.

Age group: all ages

Size of group: not more than 20

Learning goal: making contact in an unfamiliar group

Every second player converses for five minutes with her or his neighbor on the left.

One by one players introduce themselves to the whole group, in any way they choose.

Every player converses with another whom she or he finds sympathetic.

Possible extension: everyone introduces to the group the person she or he has just met.

What to watch out for:

Who chooses a partner? Who is chosen?
What do people consider important to describe about themselves—name, family situation, age, status, hobbies, interest in the group, feelings, anxieties?
What *don't* they tell?
Who talks for a long time, loudly, fluently, hesitantly, clearly, or coherently?

Warning:

It's generally unwise to collect and analyze with the group observations on individuals' behavior immediately after this game. Being challenged too soon often intimidates members of the group so badly that it's impossible to continue working with them. Some people may be intimidated by having to speak in front of a large group or by having to choose a partner they like.

7 Introducing Yourself and Getting Acquainted
Exchanging group experiences

Age group: teenagers and adults with previous group experience

Size of group: 8–20

Learning goal: to respond to another person so that you can report to others what she or he says

Players form pairs, introduce themselves to each other, and give an account of a positive and/or negative experience they have had in a group.

Partners then introduce each other to the group as a whole, referring to what the other has just said.

Every pair then joins with another pair to discuss the possibilities and difficulties of reciprocal introduction.

If it seems worthwhile, the group as a whole may then discuss the various experiences of the individuals and groups.

What to watch out for:

Who chooses a partner to talk to? Who is chosen?
Who talks for a long time, loudly, fluently, hesitantly, clearly, or coherently?
How precisely are the partner's remarks reported? Are there omissions, additions, or shifts of emphasis? Which players correct their partners when they feel they are being misrepresented?

Warning:

It's generally unwise to collect and analyze with the group observations on individuals' behavior immediately after this game. Being challenged too soon often intimidates members of the group so badly that it's impossible to continue working with them. Some people may be intimidated by having to speak in front of a large group or having to choose a partner.

Age group: teenagers and adults

Size of group: 8–20

Learning goal: to respond to another person so that you can report to others what she or he says. You need to express your expectations and misgivings so that they can be taken into consideration in the course of group discussion

Players form pairs, introduce themselves to each other, and express their expectations and misgivings concerning the group session.

Partners then introduce each other to the group as a whole, referring to what the other has just said.

Every pair joins with another pair to discuss the possibilities and difficulties of reciprocal introduction.

If it seems worthwhile, the group as a whole may then discuss the various expectations of individuals and groups.

What to watch out for:

Who chooses a partner? Who is chosen?

Which people are able to formulate their true expectations and misgivings?

Who talks for a long time, loudly, fluently, hesitantly, clearly, or coherently?

How precisely are each partner's remarks reported? Are there omissions, additions, or shifts of emphasis?

Which players correct their partners when they feel they are being misrepresented?

Warning:

It's generally unwise to collect and analyze with the group observations on individuals' behavior immediately after this game. Being challenged too soon often intimidates members of the group so badly that it's impossible to continue working with them. Some people may be intimidated by having to speak in front of a large group or having to choose a partner.

Age group:	teenagers and adults
Size of group:	8–20
Materials:	half as many pieces of string as there are participants, all the same color and length
Learning goal:	to respond to another person so that you can report to others what she or he says. You need to express your expectations and misgivings so that they can be taken into consideration in the course of group discussion

The game leader holds the bundle of strings in his hand, with the ends protruding on either side so that no one can see which end is attached to which. Each participant takes an end, and in this way the group is divided into pairs who are "strung together."

The "strung" partners talk to each other for a fixed period of time. Possible topics: expectations, wishes, anxieties, problems, plans.

Finally the partners introduce each other to the group.

What to watch out for:

Who talks for a long time, loudly, fluently, hesitantly, clearly, or coherently?

How precisely are each partner's remarks reported? Are there omissions, additions, or shifts of emphasis?

Which players correct their partners when they feel they are being misrepresented?

Warning:

It's generally unwise to collect and analyze with the group observations on individuals' behavior immediately after this game.
Being challenged too soon often intimidates members of the group
so badly that it's impossible to continue working with them. Some
people may be intimidated by having to speak in front of a large
group. However, this game is easier than the three before it
(Games 6, 7, and 8) since it does not involve choosing partners.

Age group: all ages

Size of group: 8–20

Materials: paper and crayons

Learning goal: to respond to another person so that you can
                  report to others what she or he says

Draw lots for partners (for example with pieces of string).
    Everyone draws a portrait of her or his partner.
    Everyone interviews her or his partner with certain pre-arranged
questions, such as:
—What would you take with you to a desert island? Why that
    particularly?
—If you were an animal, what kind would you like to be? Why that
    one particularly?
—What would you do with $10,000? Why?
    Partners introduce each other to the group as a whole, using the
answers given.

11 Introducing Yourself and Getting Acquainted
Snailshell

Age group: teenagers

Size of group: 8–20

Players form pairs. One partner crawls into a snailshell, in other words rolls up into a ball, figuratively shuts her- or himself off from the rest. The partner then tries to get her or him to "come out of your shell." Use both verbal and nonverbal means. Partners then change roles.

Partners discuss their expectations concerning the group session.

Partners introduce one another to the group as a whole.

Each pair joins with another pair (chosen spontaneously) to discuss the following questions for a limited time:
—What was noticeable about the introductions?
—How easy or difficult were the reciprocal introductions?

What to watch out for:

What means are used to entice the partner out of the snailshell?
Do players choose partners of the same or the opposite sex?
Who takes the initiative, particularly in mixed-sex pairs?

Warning:

Partners of the same sex often manifest a fear of physical contact, which ought to be discussed.

Duration:	about ½ hour
Age group:	older children, teenagers, and adults
Size of group:	paper and pencils
Learning goal:	making contact in an unfamiliar group

Participants write their first names in block letters on pieces of paper. They then look for other players who have names or nicknames beginning with any of the letters of their own first names. When they find appropriate names they write them crossword fashion below their own:

```
P A U L
E N   E
T N   N
E E   N
R     Y
```

When everyone has finished the players form a circle and are given consecutive numbers. As the numbers are assigned, each player tries to identify the players whose names she or he has written down by noting their numbers next to their names.

Everyone introduces her- or himself to the group by name once more.

What to watch out for:

How is contact made—spontaneously, hesitantly, or nervously?

13 Introducing Yourself and Getting Acquainted
Distinctive features I

(Drawing conclusions about someone from a picture drawn by the person)

Duration: 1½–2 hours

Age group: teenagers and adults

Size of group: 8–10

Materials: sheets of paper about 5 × 5 inches, felt pens and, if available, an opaque projector

Learning goal: self-representation through drawing

Players draw pictures of themselves on small pieces of paper, in which they try to characterize themselves by distinctive identifying features.

The drawings are shown to the group, if possible by using an opaque projector.

Players comment on their own drawings one by one.

Then the other players attribute certain qualities to the artist:

—What nickname could the artist have?

—What kind of job could she or he have apart from her or his real one?

—What hobbies might she or he have?

—How might she or he be expected to behave during the group session?

The group discusses the various suggested attributes.

What to watch out for:

Which players hesitate to begin their drawings and are unsure of themselves?

How are the drawings judged—aggressively, hesitantly, harshly, or kindly?

Warning:

Adults often find it difficult to represent themselves and to act spontaneously.

(Attributing a picture to its artist)

Duration: 1 hour

Age group: teenagers and adults

Size of group: 8–10

Materials: small sheets of paper, felt pens and, if available, an opaque projector

Learning goal: self-representation through drawing

Players draw pictures of themselves on small pieces of paper, in which they try to characterize themselves by distinctive identifying features.

The drawings are numbered consecutively, and a list of the numbers put on the wall.

The drawings are shown to the group, if possible using an opaque projector.

Each member of the group writes down on her or his own sheet of paper which picture she or he thinks was drawn by which person (it's best if the pictures are shown one at a time, so everyone has time to make a decision about the identity of the artist).

Each member of the group writes her or his choices beside the appropriate number in the list. The results are discussed—for instance, if the same choices recur.

The artists explain what they wanted their drawings to express.

Warning:

Adults often find it difficult to represent themselves and to act spontaneously.

(Assessing people by the pictures they choose)

Duration: 1½–2 hours

Age group: teenagers and adults

Size of group: 10–12

Materials: newspapers, scissors, thumb tacks, paper, and pencils

Each player selects a newspaper picture that she or he likes. The pictures are pinned on the wall.

Players write down the qualities they would attribute to each person, judging by the picture she or he has chosen:

—What nickname could this person have?

—What kind of job could she or he have apart from her or his real one?

—What hobbies might she or he have?

—How might she or he be expected to behave during the group session?

The group sits in a circle and each player reads out her or his associations with each picture.

The group discusses the results—are the associations consistent, or do some pictures suggest different things to different people?

Possible variation:

Players choose pictures they *don't* like.

What to watch out for:

Does any member's character or role in relation to the group seem to be determined during this early encounter?

Warning:

Associations can sometimes be shocking, so it's important that this game be thoroughly discussed and put into perspective.

Duration: 1 hour

Age group: teenagers and adults

Size of group: 8–10

Learning goal: consciously making judgments on the basis of a single remark

One player stands in front of the group for two minutes and *then* says whatever comes into her or his head.

The other players attribute certain qualities to this person:
—What nickname could this person have?
—What kind of job could she or he have apart from her or his real one?
—What hobbies might she or he have?
—How might she or he be expected to behave during the group session?

What to watch out for:

What kind of remarks are made? How are they made?
Is there a correlation between speech and physical expression?

Discussion aids:

How well-defined is the picture that emerges from the associations?

Warning:

For players unaccustomed to public speaking this initial verbal self-representation may be alarming and cause insecurity.

II. Communication and Group Formation

Communication and Group Formation

Communication means every kind of behavior in all areas of human life, for instance speech (words, intonation, pace, pauses), laughter, sighing, mimicry, gesture, posture. It's impossible *not* to behave; both words and silence convey information to those around you.

By interaction we mean reciprocal communication between two or more people. Every interaction has a verbal and a nonverbal aspect. Factual information is conveyed verbally, but statements about the nature of a relationship are often made nonverbally. "A gesture or expression tells us more about what another person thinks of us than hundreds of words," writes sociologist Paul Watzlawick.* Since this very form of communication is not generally considered important and therefore not actively developed, we often find it difficult to communicate nonverbally and even more difficult to talk about such behavior. Talking about both verbal and nonverbal behavior, in other words *communicating about* the how of *communication*, has been described by Watzlawick as *metacommunication* (*meta* in the sense of the Greek prefix meaning *to be about something*).

The Communication and Group Formation games are intended to allow players to practice ways of behaving, especially on the nonverbal level. The games should extend the possibilities of experience touched on in the Introduction games. Within this new and to some extent unfamiliar territory, members of the group should come to find which forms of communication are possible for them.

*Watzlawick, Paul, Beavin, Jane H., and Jackson, Don D. *Pragmatics of Human Communication*. New York: W. W. Norton, 1967.

Games can have the following objectives:
—to show and formulate emotions;
—to recognize the value of speech for releasing pent-up emotions;
—cooperation;

—to recognize different forms of communication in the behavior of group members.

In order to be systematic we have arranged "feedback" games into two categories:

In the Communication and Group Formation games one group member tells another how the latter's behavior affects her or him. In the Identification and Empathy games the group tells one member how her or his behavior affects the group.

Dangers, limits, practical tips:

Before using any game the group leader must assess the group's potential for communication. Many of the introduction games provide clues. The leader should consider such questions as:

—How do members of the group define their own roles?

—What do they overestimate, underestimate, distort, or omit?

The group leader should encourage and permit only as much unfamiliar experience as each individual member of the group can cope with without seriously endangering her or his identity.

It is advisable to pay attention to mime and gesture used in these games—is it nervous, tense, masquerade-like, uncertain, relaxed, or free? Nonverbal forms of expression often produce a different effect from what the sender intended. This is especially true with adults; since these games may cause more difficulties in adult groups they should be chosen carefully.

Age group:	all ages
Size of group:	12–20
Materials:	consecutively numbered pieces of paper for all players
Learning goal:	establishment of nonverbal contact and understanding

Members of the group sit in a circle with a volunteer in the middle. Each player in the circle draws a piece of paper with a number on it and keeps it concealed from the others.

The player in the middle calls out a number, for instance 16. Player 16 then calls out two numbers, for instance 11 and 17.

The players with the numbers 11 and 17 now have to change places, while the player in the center tries to anticipate them and take one of their places. Since players 11 and 17 don't know each other's numbers, they must first establish an understanding without the player in the middle noticing. If the player in the middle is successful, the player who loses a place must go into the center.

What to watch out for:

How is contact established?
Is it more difficult to make yourself understood or to understand others?

Warning:

The game leader should take part in the game to help integrate outsiders.

Duration: 15 minutes

Age group: all ages

Size of group: 10–20

Learning goal: establishment of nonverbal contact

All players move freely about the room. The game leader calls out a number, such as "Atom three" or "Atom eleven." The players must immediately join together in groups of three, eleven, etc. Anyone left over is eliminated. The game continues until only two players remain. The aim in a second round of the game is to eliminate these two as early as possible.

What to watch out for:

Which group members are successful? How do they succeed?
Which ones allow themselves to be excluded?
How does the group react to these two phenomena?

Age group: all ages

Size of group: 11–21 (i.e., an odd number)

Learning goal: to signal the desire for contact through mime

The "smaller half" (i.e., 10 out of 21) of the players sit on chairs arranged in a circle; one chair remains empty. The other players stand, one behind each chair, their hands behind their backs. The player behind the empty chair winks at one of the seated players. The latter attempts to jump up and sit on the empty chair. If the person standing behind the seated player who is winked at can prevent her or him from running away in time, she or he has to remain in place.

The seated and standing players change places.

What to watch out for:

What is the starting position—who sits down in order to be winked at (chosen)? Who stands? Is it mainly boys or girls who sit down?
How clearly is contact established?
Is any one person chosen several times?
How is the partner prevented from leaving?

Discussion aids:

In a group which has been together for some time the idea of possession may be taken up.

Warning:

The game leader should take part to help integrate outsiders into the game. The game may arouse anxieties because it is a kind of sociogram of the group.

Age group: children and teenagers, possibly adults

Size of group: 12–20
Materials: 2 blindfolds; 4 large wooden tables (if available)

Learning goal: orientation blindfolded

All players sit in a circle. Four large, solid wooden tables are placed in the middle (if these are not avilable, observers may stand in the middle in a smaller circle, forming a solid "wall").

Two players are blindfolded. One of them has to catch the other within a certain time (two to three minutes). Both must be touching the tables or "wall" in some way all the time (they may not leave the circle). The onlookers must keep quiet!

The "seeker" may shout "Mary, where are you?" three times. The player she or he is trying to catch must answer in some way (by speaking, whistling, hissing, etc.).

5 Communication and Group Formation
The Johnson family

Age group: all ages

Size of group: 12, 16, or 20

Materials: paper and pencils

A number of small cards, depending on the number of participants, is marked with family names and positions. Each family has four members (and four cards), for instance "Father Johnson," "Mother Johnson," "Daughter Johnson," and "Son Johnson."

The cards are mixed up and distributed among the players. When the game leader gives the command, everyone moves about the room trading cards with other players.

At another sign from the game leader—a gong or a shout—all the members of each family must find each other and sit down on one chair: Father Johnson at the bottom, then Mother Johnson, then son and daughter. The family that is last to sit down is eliminated. Communication may be verbal or nonverbal.

Variation:

The families may have animal names, such as "Cat family," "Cuckoo," or "Gorilla," and communicate with each other in "animal language."

What to watch out for:

How quickly do families find each other? Do players actively look for "their" families or do they simply stand and shout out the family name?

Does any one player act as the nucleus of a whole family?

How do players react to sitting on top of one another; are they relaxed or tense?

Age group:	all ages
Size of group:	8–20
Learning goal:	everyone gets the chance to direct the group in a communal activity on her or his own initiative. Players learn that they are all capable of leading the group for a time with their own ideas and encouragement

The game leader starts telling a story about some people moving about on the beach. The group carries out the actions described, such as walking, hopping, playing at soldiers. When the narrator says "low tide" all players have to sit on the floor. The last to sit down continues the story. When "high tide" occurs in the story everyone has to get off the floor altogether, for example by climbing onto a chair or a table. Whoever is last, or sits on the floor by mistake, has to continue the narrative.

7 Communication and Group Formation
Everybody do what John does

Age group:	children and teenagers, possibly adults
Size of group:	6–20
Materials:	a hat
Learning goal:	anyone can lead the group in a communal activity using her or his own ideas

Players move about the room. One player wears the hat and makes a particular movement, such as walking in an odd way. All the rest of the players imitate the movement until the hat-wearer places the hat on someone else's head. This player then demonstrates a movement, and so on. If a player can't think of a movement at once the others simply imitate her or his posture or expression.

What to watch out for:

What kind of movements do players invent—slow, fast, simple, complicated, standing still or walking?
Which players make the movement by themselves, and which ones use partners?
How soon is the hat handed on to someone else?

Age group: teenagers and adults

Size of group: 8–20

Materials: radio, tape recorder, or record player

Players attempt to drown out a noise, such as a radio, by making a noise themselves, beginning quietly and gradually getting as loud as possible. Finally they grow quiet again, slowly.

Variation:

The game can also be played without an external noise; the players drown out an imaginary one.

What to watch out for:

Who takes the initiative in making a noise?
Do all members of the group play an equal part?
What position do players adopt while shouting—relaxed, tense, looking at other players or at the floor?

9 Communication and Group Formation
The walk

Age group: all ages

Size of group: 10–20

The game leader tells a story about a walk. He describes everything that happens on the walk and accompanies the narrative with gestures and movements which the group has to copy, for example:

—walking along the street: slap your thighs rhythmically

—wind in the grass: rub your palms together

—crossing a bridge: beat your chest with your fists

—jumping over a ditch: first drum on your thighs quickly—pause—then slap your knee

—climbing a tree: place your fists alternately one on top of the other while you stand up slowly and then climb onto a chair

—on the lookout: shade your eyes with your hand

Age group: all ages

Size of group: 8–20

Each player finds a partner. Partners stand facing each other with enough room between them to move their arms and legs freely. They begin to move slowly, each carrying out a mirror image of the other's movements.

The game is repeated with different partners.

What to watch out for:

Which partner takes the lead?

When and how do partners exchange leadership?

What are their movements like—angular, disjointed, or flowing or graceful?

Which players perform acrobatic feats in order to make it impossible for their partners to imitate them (competition)?

Age group: all ages

Size of group: 6–14

Learning goal: coming to a group decision

Players stand in a circle. Everyone watches and imitates the movements of the player standing opposite, until the whole group is carrying out the same movement; at the same time everyone tries to introduce new movements.

Players lie in a circle with their heads toward the center, eyes closed. They attempt to communicate by knocking on the floor, singing notes, playing word games, word associations, and so on. Everyone tries to introduce new themes at the same time as she or he is listening to the others and trying to come to a group idea.

What to watch out for:

Who has ideas for movements and who doesn't?
From which players can and will the group take ideas for movements?
What does this depend on—the idea or the identity of the inventor?
Do all members of the group play an equal part?
Do players try to show off or do they work together to develop an idea?

Warning:

Members of the group who did not make a contribution or who could not make their ideas understood will feel particularly left out. The group should be told beforehand that word associations are not to be commented on or criticized.

Age group: all ages

Size of group: 8–20

Each player finds a partner. The game leader gives the following instructions: "Use your hands to make gestures of aggression or friendship toward each other. If you want you can close your eyes. Do it again with different partners."

What to watch out for:

Which players make only gestures of friendship or only gestures of aggression?
Toward which players are only gestures of friendship or of aggression made?
Which players are sensitive to the fact that only friendly or aggressive gestures are being made to them?

Warning:

Outsiders become particularly apparent in this game because it combines choice of partners and choice of behavior.

13 Communication and Group Formation
Contrary game I

Age group: all ages

Size of group: 8–16

Two groups of equal size stand facing each other a few yards apart. The game leader gives them the following instructions one after another or alternately:
—Communicate with each other verbally as groups.
—As individuals, communicate verbally with a partner in the other group.
—Establish eye contact with a partner in the other group.
—Establish contact with a partner in the other group by gesture only.

What to watch out for:

Who makes contact with whom?
Who can't find a partner at a distance?
Do participants find one particular method of communication more difficult?

Age group: all ages

Size of group: 8–20

Players divide into two groups.

One group is a long way away and the other group has to attract its attention.

The members of one group are blind and the others have to make contact with them.

What to watch out for:

Do the players make contact with each other individually or as groups?

Age group: all ages

Size of group: 8–15

The group has to produce a machine. First players choose an inventor who has to come up with the idea for the machine, and an engineer, and several workers who are to build the machine according to the inventor's instructions out of the rest of the players. The machine is then set in motion; the players accompany and punctuate their movements with noises.

What to watch out for:

How are roles allocated?

Age group: all ages

Size of group: 8–14

Materials: a rope

A rope is placed on the floor in a circle. Everyone takes hold of it as if it were a large circular glass plate. The "plate" has to be carried round the room, lifted up and put down carefully.

The rope is changed into the shape of a rectangle, a square, etc., by the group acting jointly.

What to watch out for:

Are the communal movements awkward or smooth?
Who determines the speed of the group's movement?
Who initiates the change of shapes?

17 Communication and Group Formation
Photo lotto

Duration:	½ hour
Age group:	older children, teenagers, and adults
Size of group:	several small groups of 4 to 6, with at least one observer to a group
Materials:	one photograph per player, each cut into about 20 pieces

Players divide into groups of four to six, sitting at round tables. The photograph pieces belonging to the players in any one group are put on the table and mixed up.

Everyone has to assemble a picture. Players may only take pieces from the table. If a player picks up a piece belonging to another photograph she or he must put it back on the table. No one may speak during the game, and no one may intervene directly in another player's work.

At least one observer follows the activities of each group.

What to watch out for:

Who keeps pieces longer than necessary before putting them back on the table?
Which players watch what the others are doing?

Age group: all ages

Size of group: any number divisible by 4

Materials: newspapers

Learning goal: each player's ideas enrich the work of the
                    group; the ideas of others can be taken over
                    and developed

Each group of four has to tear an animal shape out of newspaper.
One player starts and hands the paper on to the next player when
she or he has completed one part. Each player has one turn.

Possible variations:

No one may speak during the game.
Only single words may be spoken.

What to watch out for:

Which players force the group to carry out their ideas?
Does a power struggle emerge within the group in this game?

Age group: teenagers and adults, possibly children

Learning goal: to articulate something collectively. Everyone has the chance to change the statement, but each contribution has to follow from what was said before

The group sits in a circle and forms collective sentences. The first player says a word, the neighbor on the left adds another, the neighbor on the left a third and so on, to a period.

What to watch out for:

What kind of sentences are formed?
Do all the players feel equally involved?
Does anyone cheat by using only expletives?

Discussion aids:

This game is particularly suitable for articulating collective unease, annoyance, or aggression.

Duration: ½ hour

Age group: teenagers and adults

Size of group: 8–20

Players converse in pairs for fifteen minutes on a topic. Afterward each partner tries to reproduce the other's opinion. Finally each assesses how accurately her or his opinion was represented.

What to watch out for:

How accurately is the partner's opinion reproduced—are there omissions, additions, or shifts of emphasis?
How do players use the opportunity to correct their partners?

21 Communication and Group Formation
Advertisement story

Age group: all ages

Size of group: 6–10

Materials: adjectives taken from an advertisement

The group is given a number of adjectives, taken from a single advertisement if possible, which it uses to invent a story.

What to watch out for:

Who has ideas and how are they expressed—as a suggestion to the others, a means of self-expression, or a means of self-assertion?

Age group: teenagers and adults

Size of group: several small groups of 4–6

Each group conducts a nonsense debate on a theme of its own choice, with players choosing their own roles.

What to watch out for:

Who has ideas and how are they expressed—as a suggestion to the others, a means of self-expression, or a means of self-assertion?
Do players take up other people's ideas, or do they not respond to each other?

23 Communication and Group Formation
Communication game

Duration:	45 minutes–1 hour
Age group:	teenagers and adults
Size of group:	any number between 9 and 21 that is divisible by 3
Learning goal:	listening

The group divides into groups of three. The game leader sets a theme for discussion, or the groups themselves choose themes. Two players discuss the theme, but each has to repeat what the other has just said before replying. The third member of the group acts as observer. The game is repeated until everyone has been observer once.

What to watch out for:

How do players reproduce each other's arguments—precisely, inaccurately, sympathetically, or as a means of self-expression?

Age group: all ages

Size of group: 4–20

Materials: building blocks of various shapes and sizes

Learning goal: deciding when and how an individual can
                  contribute to group activity

The players sit in a circle. Each is given the same number of building blocks (three to five). There should be silence. The game is to build a communal structure in the middle of the circle. Only one player at a time may leave her or his place and put a block in position. The next player may not stand up until the last one has sat down again.

What to watch out for:

Who is first to put a block in position, and who hesitates? Why?
Do some players have difficulty placing their blocks when they want to? If so, what are the reasons for this?
Are some players aware of being impatient, or too hesitant? How do the others react to them?

Duration:	2½–3 hours
Age group:	teenagers and adults
Size of group:	several small groups of 4–6 with an observer in each group
Materials:	building blocks or Lego bricks, written instructions for each group
Learning goal:	to think through written instructions instead of following them blindly

Each small group receives the following written instructions:

You have an hour to build a city with the materials provided. It should contain: 1 factory, 1 railroad station, 3 housing projects, 3 single-family houses, 1 mansion, 1 Catholic and 1 Protestant church and 1 synagogue, 1 grade school, 1 high school, parks, 1 airport.

After the hour is up, a jury is formed with two representatives from each group. The jury has fifteen minutes to work out in the presence of the whole group criteria for judging the cities.

When the jury has pronounced judgement on the cities, the small groups discuss the results of their work among themselves. Finally there is a discussion among the group as a whole.

What to watch out for:

How well do the groups work together?

How do the groups react to the written instruction?

Do they conform to the instructions or act independently when they realize no social establishments or facilities—no stores, no restaurants, cafés, or bars, no movie houses, concert halls, or museums, no sports facilities, etc. are mentioned.

Is this omission even noticed?

What kind of criteria does the jury set up?

Discussion aids:

It should emerge that even instructions given by an authority may be incomplete or incorrect, and must be thought over before being acted upon.

Duration:	2 hours
Age group:	teenagers and adults
Size of group:	12–20 (several small groups of 3–5 players each)
Materials:	for each group: 1 pencil, 4 sheets of colored paper, 10 strips of white paper (12 × 3 inches), various cardboard boxes, 2 sheets of corrugated cardboard, 1 12-inch ruler, scissors, 1 folder, 1 roll of transparent tape, 1 tube of glue, 4 felt pens (red, blue, green, black), string, 4 jars of paint of different colors, 2 brushes, 2 sheets of wrapping paper

The following instructions are read out to the group:

Get into groups three to five players. Each group must build a tower using only the materials provided. The group may cut, fold, glue, and assemble the materials in any way you wish. However, you must obey the following rules:

—The strips of white paper must be used as they are.

—Cardboard and corrugated cardboard may be used only in strips no longer or wider than the ruler.

—The tower must be able to stand on its own base; it may not lean against a wall or any object in the room, and it may not be suspended or attached to the ceiling.

This is a competition between the groups. The towers will be judged by a jury on three points: height, stability, and originality of design. The jury will be made up of two members of each group.

The tower must be completed and ready for inspection by the jury in one hour. The jury has twenty minutes to discuss the towers in front of the whole group and come to a decision.

When you've finished your tower, please send your first jury member to meet the representatives from the other groups.

What to watch out for:

Which players dominate their groups?
Is the tower a joint effort or the work of an individual?
Which players are not included in the building of the tower?
How closely do the groups cohere?

Duration: 2 hours

Age group: teenagers and adults

Size of group: several small groups of 4–8 players each

Materials: as in "Building a tower I" or any other materials
                 preferred

The small groups are given half an hour to build structures such as towers from the given materials. The game is repeated three times, once under each of the following conditions:
—*Only* verbal communication allowed.
—*No* verbal communication allowed.
—Communication through single words only.
Each group chooses an observer who will report her or his observations in the ensuing discussion.

What to watch out for:

Which form of communication did the groups find hardest?
Which players dominate their groups?
Are the towers a joint effort or the work of an individual?
Which players are not included in the building of the towers?
How closely do the groups cohere?

28 Communication and Group Formation
Group painting

Age group:	all ages
Size of group:	4–20
Materials:	paper and colors (wallpaper, wrapping paper, or scrap paper; felt pens, wax crayons, or finger paints)
Learning goal:	to decide when and how the individual can contribute to group activity; interpreting, assimilating, and developing nonverbal statements made by others

The group sits around the piece of paper. No one is allowed to speak. Everyone contributes to the production of a group painting as often and as much as she or he wants to.

What to watch out for:

Who starts the painting, who holds back, why?
Who initiates new developments, who continues?
Who destroys work, who makes changes?
How many people are painting at once?
Are there intervals when no one is painting?
Who ends them and how?

Duration: 1 hour

Age group: teenagers and adults

Size of group: several small groups of 5–8 players with an observer in each group

This game is intended as a mime, but it may also be played using words.

Each group has to "make a movie," in other words devise and act out a plot (such as a detective story, a Western, a domestic comedy, a revue) in front of the group as a whole. The groups decide either to all make the same kind of movie, in which case the game may be a competition among the groups, or to make different kinds of movies.

Roles are allocated: scriptwriter, director, cameraman, male and female lead, etc. The groups rehearse separately. Later the observers describe the rehearsals.

When one group is performing, members of other groups may be called upon to act as scenery or extras.

Variation:

If several groups are taking part, one could "make a movie" without first allocating fixed roles.

What to watch out for:

Which players dominate their groups?
Is the movie a joint effort or the work of an individual?
Which players are not included in the work?
How closely do the groups cohere?

Duration: 3 hours

Age group: teenagers and adults

Size of group: 2 or 3 small groups of 8 players, each with an observer

Materials: paper, pencil, and instructions for each player

Learning goal: to recognize the advantages of group work over individual work

Players form groups of about eight. Each group receives the following written instructions:

Name:
Group:
You are members of a space team which had originally planned to meet up with a mother spacecraft on the surface of the moon. As a result of technical difficulties, however, your spacecraft has been forced to land about 200 miles away from the meeting place. A lot of equipment on board was damaged in landing. Since your survival depends on your reaching the mother ship, you have to choose the most vital of the available equipment for making the 200-mile journey. Below you will find a list of fifteen things that were not damaged. Your task is to arrange them in order of their importance for the journey. Write 1 beside the most important thing, 2 beside the second most important, and so on.

1 box of matches
1 tube of food concentrate
15 yards of nylon rope
30 yards of parachute rope
1 portable heater
2 pistols
1 box of powdered milk
2 10-gallon oxygen cylinders

1 astronomical chart (moon constellation)
1 rubber dinghy, automatically inflatable, with bottles of CO$_2$
1 magnetic compass
5 gallons of water
signal flares (ignitable in vacuum)
1 first-aid box with syringes
1 telecommunication receiver and transmitter with solar batteries

In this exercise we use a model situation to act out our ability to make decisions, to test the most sensible way of making decisions, and to see what difficulties may arise in the decision-making process.

1. Individual decision: Each of you works out your individual solution to the problem, which you write down on paper and hand in. You may if you wish keep copies of your suggested solutions.

2. Group decision: The aim here is a joint decision acceptable to each member of the group. This means everyone in the group must agree to the order assigned to each of the fifteen objects necessary for survival. It's impossible for all of you to agree on every point; but you must attempt to make decisions that every member of the group can at least partially accept.

3. Each group chooses three representatives who are felt best able to handle the decision. Then the three representatives from each group meet as a whole and come to a joint "expert" decision. The rest of the players may listen.

To end the game, all the various solutions are compared with each other, and with the solution of NASA experts, who gave the following order: Oxygen cylinders, water, astronomical chart, food concentrate, telecommunication apparatus, nylon rope, first-aid box, parachute rope, rubber dinghy, signal flares, pistols, powdered milk, heater, magnetic compass, matches.

What to watch out for:

How does the discussion work—is it objective or emotional; is there assertion of individual interests or negotiation and compromise?
Do the groups set out to reach majority decisions?
Are all the players involved?
Do the professions and status of players affect decision-making?

Duration:	1 hour
Age group:	teenagers and adults
Size of group:	several small groups of 5–7 each
Materials:	crepe paper, newspapers, sewing pins, glue or tape, etc.

Each group chooses a fashion designer and a model. With the materials provided (each group must have the same) they make an outfit for the model according to the designer's specifications.

The model is then presented to a jury and the group as a whole. The jury or the group judges them.

What to watch out for:

How are the principal roles allocated?
What criteria are used for judging the models?

Duration: 1 hour

Age group: teenagers and adults

Size of group: several small groups of 5-7 players

Materials: 5–7 photos per group, cut out of magazines

Each group has a given amount of time to think up an article to fit the photos. Each group then chooses a "reporter" to present the story to the rest of the players. This game may be a competition between groups, with a jury awarding points.

What to watch out for:

Are all the players equally involved in making up the story?
Do the groups devise original ideas, or just reproduce the usual kind of magazine story?

Duration:	1 hour
Age group:	teenagers and adults
Size of group:	several small groups of 5–7 players
Materials:	written instructions for each player
Learning goal:	reflecting reality in a game

Because the market for its products is shrinking the Miller Company, Inc. has to lay off one of its workers. The president, vice president, and two members of the employees' union must decide which of three workers should be laid off:

—A 50-year-old man whose work is mediocre. Married, with two children who have already left home.

—A 30-year-old man, divorced, with one child that he has to support. He leads an irregular life and often arrives late for work, but his work is brilliant.

—A 22-year-old man, married, with one child. His work is average. He has made a bad impression on his superiors by his critical comments.

What to watch out for:

On what level is the decision-making conducted, objective or emotional?
What criteria are used for making the decision?
Do objective arguments play an important role?
Does individual self-assertion play an important role?

Duration:	1 hour
Age group:	teenagers and adults
Size of group:	6–20
Materials:	paper and pens

Each player is given a piece of paper with the name of another player on it. No one else sees the name. The players then write personal letters to the players whose names they have been given.

The letters are folded up with the name of the recipient on the outside and passed around until players find the letters addressed to themselves. Players read the letters they have received and discuss them in smaller groups. The game may be played with or without signing the letters.

What to watch out for:

What do the letters say—is it positive or negative?
How do they say it—offensively, or offering advice?
In what form can criticism be "heard" and accepted?

Warning:

The game is pointless if there is no mutual trust within the group and only banalities can be exchanged.

Duration: 1 hour

Age group: teenagers and adults

Size of group: 6–14

Materials: paper and pens

Each player draws a piece of paper which has the name of a fellow player on it. She or he writes down three impressions she or he has received of the other player.

The "letters" are collected, mixed up, and read out one after the other. The person who is being described must guess the identity of the writer.

What to watch out for:

What do the "letters" say—is it positive or negative?
How do they say it—offensively or offering advice?
In what form can criticism be heard and accepted?

Warning:

The game is pointless if there is no mutual trust within the group and only banalities can be exchanged.

Age group: teenagers and adults

Size of group: 6–12

Materials: paper and pens

One player writes down the name of another member of the group. The others take turns trying to find out whose name it is by suggesting possible characteristics of the person. The first player answers "Yes" or "No" depending on whether the suggestions are appropriate.

What to watch out for:

Which names are easy to guess?
What does it depend on (e.g., distinctive behavior)?

Warning:

A player whose name is not written down, or not until the end, may feel hurt.

Age group: all ages

Size of group: 8–20

Learning goal: finding a place within the group

All players wait outside the room. They go in one by one, in silence, each one choosing a place to "settle" which is comfortable or near to someone sympathetic. If someone they find unsympathetic comes and settles nearby, players may move away or change places. The game continues until various groups have formed.

No one may speak during the game.

What to watch out for:

Where do players settle in relation to each other and to the room? Who chooses to settle near to whom? How did the chosen person react?

How are differences of opinion resolved—by self-assertion, compromise, or resignation?

How are feelings expressed?

Discussion aids:

Difficulties, feelings, and anxieties arising out of this "settling" game must absolutely be discussed.

Warning:

It must be made clear that the result of the game does not reflect an unalterable, permanent group situation, but only a fleeting "snapshot."

Duration: 1½–2 hours

Age group: teenagers and adults

Size of group: 8–20

The female members of the group remain in the room and do something together.

The male members leave the room and have one to two minutes to decide how they want to make contact with the players in the room. They then put their plan into action.

Afterward the female group members make contact with the male group members in a different way.

Male and female players may also exchange roles: men play women and vice versa.

What to watch out for:

What method of communication is chosen—verbal, or physical?
Is the communication friendly or aggressive?
Is the group's behavior sexually determined?
How does the group define sexually determined behavior?

Discussion aids:

Sexually determined role-playing must be discussed in relation to its function in a sociocultural context.

Duration: ½ hour–45 minutes

Age group: teenagers and adults

Size of group: 8–20

Several players sit on the floor, forming a "fort." The other members of the group try to break down their team spirit without using force.

Players in the fort receive the following instructions, one after the other:

—Close together and don't let anyone in.
—Sit back and relax and talk among yourselves.
—Lie down with your heads toward the center.
—Lie down with your feet toward the center.

Possible variations:

Only female members of the group form the fort
Only male members form the fort
Male and female members form the fort

What to watch out for:

How do players form their fort—facing in or out? How do they create a team spirit?
How do the others try to capture the fort—by aggression, petition, persuasion, or argument? Individually or jointly? Do they try to break down the weakest member?
Is the behavior of participants sexually determined?

Discussion aids:

Sexually determined behavior in this game should be pointed out and discussed.

III. Observation and Perception

Observation and Perception

By observation we mean the deliberate, careful, and systematic perception of the developments and characteristics of things, events, or people. The observer aims to get to know as thoroughly as possible how things are happening in relation to particular situations. We differentiate between the observation of others and self-observation. Receiving and becoming aware of impressions aimlessly and unintentionally we call perception; perception does not involve deliberate selection.

Why have we devoted one section of our game collection to the development of observation and perception? On the whole these faculties are insufficiently cultivated, especially in relation to behavior, social interaction, and communication. Our games should help players to observe certain processes that manifest themselves in group activities on both an emotional and a physical level. It is essential to observe these processes in order to be able to talk about them, discover what lies behind them, and if necessary change them.

There are different stages in increasing your awareness, for instance: becoming aware of observation (scouting games that train the senses of smell, taste, touch, hearing, and sight are good for this); practice at perceiving several constantly changing things simultaneously. Developing the power of observation is particularly important in relation to nonverbal behavior (mime, gesture), as is the observation of voice pitch and intensity in verbal communication.

It is also necessary to direct players' attention to their own feelings and physical sensations during these games—such as any tension, headaches, or edginess they might feel. They will be better able to assess themselves if they are able not only to observe their own behavior but also to learn to sense its effect on other players. This awareness will help each person achieve a sense of belonging to the group as well as a distance from it. The ability to assess what is happening brings with it a sense of security. Players learn to perceive changes in structure and relationships within the group, and to control forms of communication and if necessary change them.

Dangers, limits, practical tips: The following points should be kept in mind and made clear to the group:

—Each person's perceptive faculty is always selective, since each of us is conditioned by social norms, prejudices, personal experience, and character. Certain modes of behavior simply go unnoticed, and others will be overemphasized. In addition, each observer's receptivity or capacity to learn is limited.

—You can influence an observed phenomenon by approaching it with fixed ideas.

—Your observations always depend on your physical state and emotional mood at the time.

Since observations are always subjective, it is absolutely essential to discuss them in the group and give everyone the opportunity to add her or his observations and objectify them. It is also a great help in many of the games to make certain observation categories clear to all players before the game starts, so that it will be easier to make comparisons.

Of course, any group can work out and apply its own patterns for observation. One set of categories that seems particularly useful, as outlined by the American sociologist Bales,* describes twelve ways of classifying behavior within a group. These categories embrace the following areas: orientation (6 & 7), assessment (5 & 8), control (4 & 9), decision (3 & 10), tensions (2 & 11), integration (1 & 12). The behavior specified is as follows:

1. Shows solidarity, puts others before him- or herself, helps and rewards.
2. Shows lack of tension, jokes, laughs, shows satisfaction.
3. Is acquiescent, shows passive acceptance, understands, cooperates, consents.
4. Gives advice and instructions to others, assuming their autonomy.
5. Offers his opinion, judgment, interpretation; expresses feelings and desires.
6. Gives directions, information, repeats, explains, confirms.
7. Asks for directions, information, repetition, explanations, confirmation.

8. Asks for other peoples' opinions, judgments, interpretations, feelings.
9. Asks for advice, instructions, possible courses of action.
10. Contradicts, shows passive resistance, formality, refuses help.
11. Shows tension, asks for help, withdraws from the field.
12. Shows hostility, puts others down, asserts or stands up for himself.

*Bales' categories may be found in: Joseph Luft, *Group Processes: An Introduction to Group Dynamics*. 2d ed. Palo Alto, Calif.: National Press, 1970.

Age group: teenagers and adults

Size of group: 12–20

Several members of the group observe another member for a certain period—for instance, during another game—without her or him knowing it. Afterward they report their observations.

What to watch out for:

How do the observers describe the behavior of the subject?
To what extent do their observations reflect their personal relations with her or him?

Warning:

Do not choose as a subject a member who plays a particularly negative role in the group, or the observers will describe only negative behavior.

Age group: teenagers and adults

Size of group: 6–12

Learning goal: to recognize the correlation between one's profession and one's perception

Each player chooses a profession, for instance, bus driver, housewife, teacher, window cleaner, lawyer, bartender. Together they observe some everyday event—on a trip, on television, or elsewhere.

Afterward each of them writes an account of the event from her or his assumed "professional" point of view. The reports are read aloud one by one.

What to watch out for:

Do the players succeed in assuming roles, or do they simply give their own points of view?

Age group: teenagers and adults

Size of group: 8–10

One player sits in a chair with the rest of the group sitting in a semicircle round her or him. For one or two minutes the group asks the central player questions on any subject. (The time must be specified beforehand—no more than two minutes). The player in the center must answer all the questions with *lies*.

When the time is up, the next player takes a turn. Finally the group discusses observations made during the game.

What to watch out for:

How does each player behave while being questioned—physically restless, nervous, or calm, comfortable? Does she or he get into a muddle when answering, or give skillful answers?
What kind of questions does the group ask? Are some members questioned in a friendly way, some aggressively?

Discussion aids:

How does truth emerge from lies?

4 Observation and Perception
Description game I

Age group: all ages

Size of group: 10–20

Members of the group converse for a short time or play another short game, without being told what they have to do next: to sit somewhere in the room where they can't see each other, and to describe at least one of the other members.

What to watch out for:

Who describes whom?
Why are some players described frequently and others not at all?
What sort of things are described?
Do the descriptions involve judgments as well?

Age group: all ages

Size of group: 8–20

Materials: paper and pens

One member of the group is sent out of the room. The others have to write a precise description of her or him: height, color of hair and eyes, clothes and shoes, etc.

What to watch out for:

Why are some players described in detail, others vaguely?
Is there some correlation between the way a person is described and her or his position in the group?

6 Observation and Perception
Hands game II

Age group: teenagers and adults

Size of group: 8–20

The group divides into equal halves, A and B (by sex if there are equal numbers of men and women). The two groups stand facing one another; A players hold out their hands, B players study them for a certain length of time.

The B players then turn around. A players may not alter the appearance of their hands in any way at this point (with rings, etc.).

Each A player chooses a B player, stands behind her or him and holds her or his hands about three to six inches in front of the player's face. The B players have to guess whose hands they are looking at.

What to watch out for:

Who is identified? Who isn't?
How long do players take to identify the others?

Age group: teenagers and adults

Size of group: 8–20

Materials: a large cardboard screen with two eye-holes in it (it could be placed in a doorway); paper and pens or pencils

Players divide into two groups. One group stands behind the cardboard screen, and one by one its players look through the eye-holes. The other group has to try to identify the person who is looking through the holes by her or his eyes, each person writing down their guesses in sequence on a sheet of paper. The guesses are then compared.

What to watch out for:

Do the guesses vary very much from one another?
Why are some players not identified at all?

8 Observation and Perception
What's changed?

Age group: all ages

Size of group: 8–20

The group divides into two rows facing each other. For one minute each player studies the appearance of the player opposite. Then everyone turns around so they can't see one another, and each player makes three changes in her or his appearance. Players then turn back to face one another and try to figure out how their partners have changed.

What to watch out for:

Do the players make slight or obvious changes in their appearance?
Why do some players find it difficult to see changes in their partners?

Age group: all ages

Size of group: 8–20

Materials: two wooden spoons and a blindfold

One player is blindfolded. She or he takes a wooden spoon in each hand and stands in the center of the circle of players. Another player stands in front of the blindfolded one in any position she or he chooses, such as crouching, bending, kneeling, or standing on tiptoe with hands in the air.

The blindfolded player has to touch the other with the wooden spoons and try to identify her or him. If the "toucher" is successful the "touched" player is blindfolded and the game is repeated.

What to watch out for:

How are people recognized—by their clothes or physical features?
How does the "toucher" touch—hesitantly, confidently?
How does the "touched" person react—in a tense, ticklish, or relaxed manner?

Discussion aids:

It's absolutely essential that any feelings of unease arising out of this game be taken seriously and discussed, not as individual problems but in relation to the sociocultural situation.

10 Observation and Perception
Sheet game

Age group: all ages

Size of group: 8–20

Materials: one sheet for each player

Each player puts a sheet over her or his head. They all walk round the room in silence and try to identify each other by feeling and touching. When two players have recognized each other they drop out of the game.

What to watch out for:

How are people recognized—by their clothes or physical features?
How does the toucher touch—hesitantly, confidently?
How does the touched person react—in a tense, ticklish, or relaxed manner?

Discussion aids:

It's absolutely essential that any feelings of unease arising out of this game be taken seriously and discussed, not as individual problems but in relation to the sociocultural situation.

Age group: all ages

Size of group: 12–20

Materials: a blanket

Players stand in a circle facing outward, with their eyes closed. The game leader moves them into different positions in the circle so that no one knows any more where the others are standing. The game leader then puts one of them in the center, makes her or him crouch down, and covers her or him with a blanket. At a given signal the others turn around.

Who is first to realize who is missing?

If necessary the missing person can be touched.

What to watch out for:

How long does it take to discover who's missing?
How many people work it out?

Discussion aids:

The speed with which a person is missed depends partly on her or his position in the group. So it's not a good idea to choose players who are conspicuous for their positive or negative behavior. On the other hand this game will emphasize the position of outsiders, who are easily overlooked. The reasons for any "oversight" should be discussed.

12 Observation and Perception
Pipe up, Johnny!

Age group: all ages

Size of group: 8–20

Materials: a blindfold

Players sit in a circle. One is blindfolded. She or he sits on someone's lap and says, "Pipe up, Johnny!" The other player must respond (up to three times) in a disguised voice. If the blindfolded player can't guess her or his identity she or he must go to another player and try again. Otherwise the player whose identity is guessed is blindfolded in turn.

Variation:

The blindfolded player may touch the other.

Age group: all ages

Size of group: 8–20

Materials: a blindfold

Players stand in a circle. One is blindfolded, placed in the center, and turned round several times so that she or he loses any sense of direction. Then the player points anywhere she or he chooses. The player pointed to whispers a short sentence to the blindfolded player, who then has to try to identify her or him. If the blindfolded player fails, she or he must point in another direction. If she or he succeeds, the player who is identified becomes the blindfolded one.

14 Observation and Perception
"Telephone"

Age group: all ages

Size of group: 8–20

The group sits in a circle. One player begins by whispering something in her or his neighbor's ear. The neighbor repeats it to the next neighbor, and so on. When the whisper has gone all round the circle the final version is compared with the original.

Variation:

Instead of a whisper a short movement sequence may be passed round the circle.

Discussion aids:

The reasons why a whisper gets distorted should be made clear—ambiguity of information, careless listening, selective listening, association instead of listening, or wanting to force everything into a pattern.

Age group: all ages

Size of group: 8–20

One player sets a rumor in circulation; the next player takes it for
the truth and adds further speculation to it. When all the players
have taken a turn the final version of the rumor is compared with
the original.

16 Observation and Perception
Story chain

Age group: all ages

Size of group: 6–20

Several players leave the room. One of the players remaining in the room tells a story, not too short and full of detail. One of the listeners then gets a player from outside and tells her or him the story. This player gets another player from outside, tells her or him the story, and so on. The final version of the story is compared with the original.

Variation:

Instead of making up a story, the first player may read aloud a detailed text, which then has to be reproduced.

Discussion aids:

The reasons why information gets distorted must be made clear—subjective perception and interpretation of events, leading to corresponding alterations; inadequate control of the communication medium; information not understood as the narrator intended.

Age group: all ages

Size of group: 8–20

Learning goal: to assess the ambiguity of information

Several players leave the room. Those remaining behind devise a mime which can be performed without props, for instance elephants swimming at the dentist, changing the baby, etc.

One player is brought from outside and told to watch the scene carefully so as to be able to repeat it. The players from outside are brought in one by one to watch and perform the mime. When everyone has seen and performed the mime the original is repeated. The mime may not be explained during the course of the game.

Discussion aids:

The reasons why information gets distorted must be made clear—subjective perception and interpretation of events, leading to corresponding alterations; inadequate control of the communication medium; information not understood as the performer intended.

Age group: all ages

Size of group: 6–20

Players sit in a circle and take consecutive numbers. Players with even numbers are "dumb," those with odd numbers are "deaf." The deaf players can talk but can't hear; their neighbors can hear but not speak—they have to make themselves understood by gestures. The deaf players talk to the dumb ones, who have to reply with movements.

IV. Identification and Empathy

Identification and Empathy

Empathy is the ability to project yourself into other people's personalities, to understand them from their own situation, to be aware of their attitudes and recognize their needs. It does not necessarily involve sharing their convictions, standards, and values, or approving of their actions.

By identification we mean discovering in another person feelings, anxieties, modes of behavior, or experiences the same as your own. This enables you to understand the other person and respond to her or him accordingly.

Certain conditions are necessary for identification and empathy: emotional stability, a sense of being under no pressure, and the certainty of being able to sustain your own role.

The games in this category should help players to become aware of other people's points of view and understand their needs, and so to widen and deepen their field of communication. Players can reach this goal by learning to express their own feelings, opinions, criticism, dissatisfaction, appreciation, or recognition, each to varying degrees in the individual games. After this learning process players will be better able to respond to the ideas and behavior of other members of the group, to predict other people's reactions to their own behavior, and to adjust their behavior accordingly.

An additional learning goal is to question and if necessary change the standards and values of behavior previously agreed on in the group (the ability to abandon roles)—this should make tensions within the group more tolerable. It is also valuable to learn that verbal and nonverbal statements are often incompatible, that in fact they usually contradict one another. Developing the ability to empathize or identify with others will enable players to assess their position in a group and also to recognize other members for what they are without forcing them into roles.

Dangers, limits, practical tips: There is one great danger with these games: people with weak egos may see here an opportunity to transfer their own problems to other people instead of accepting them themselves. The games may also encourage such people to express their own needs indirectly, through other people, without ever being fully aware of them. These people will be unable to realize themselves through games. It's difficult for them to form a relationship with another person on equal terms, since they often use other people as tools.

The abuse of identification and empathy may also appear in other forms of behavior. When someone admires the behavior of another person he may be tempted to imitate it uncritically or, if someone thinks and speaks only from the point of view of another person, his own personality desires and needs may become submerged.

When putting these games into practice it is important to explain to the group that prejudices and stereotypes limit or even prevent empathy and identification.

1 Identification and Empathy
Controlling conversation

Duration: 1 hour

Age group: teenagers and adults

Size of group: 6–20

Person A makes a true statement. Person B has to interpret what she or he has said by asking: "Do you mean that. . . ?" A answers "Yes," "No," or "To some extent," depending on how accurate she or he feels the interpretation is. B continues asking questions until A has answered "Yes" three times. (Several "To some extents" don't count.)

Afterward A and B exchange roles.

What to watch out for:

How difficult do people find it to interpret accurately what another person has said?

Do the players being questioned help the others in any way, or are they intent on answering "No" as often as possible?

Discussion aids:

Point out possible causes of difficulties in interpretation.

Age group: all ages

Size of group: 8–20

Players divide into pairs. One player in each pair closes her or his eyes and allows the other to lead her or him around the room. They then exchange roles.

The leading may be done:
—with words;
—without words but with both hands;
—without words, with one hand;
—without words, with one finger.

This exercise is a useful preparation for "Snake."

What to watch out for:

Who takes the leading role first—is it sexually determined?
Do people find it difficult to allow themselves to be led?
Do the leaders move quickly, slowly, carefully, or over-carefully?
What effect does this have on the persons they are leading?
Do players bump into one another?
How does communication work—are the verbal and nonverbal signals precise?

Warning:

Adults often find it difficult to trust someone else spontaneously.

Duration:	Impossible to say. Not too short, or players won't have a chance to get used to the touch signals. Not too long, because moving around "blindly" is tiring (especially for people with poor blood circulation)
Age group:	all ages
Size of group:	6–14
Learning goal:	to trust one another and take responsibility for one another

Players form a snake by holding onto each other's shoulders or hands. Everyone closes her or his eyes except the player at the front of the snake, who leads the others around, negotiating real or imaginary obstacles, climbing stairs, going over, round, or through things, around tight bends, sometimes crouching, sometimes on tiptoe. Signals may be given only by touch.

What to watch out for:

Who leads? Why? (When groups are just starting it may be advisable for the game leader to take the lead.)
How does he or she lead—quickly, slowly, carefully, or over-carefully?
How clearly are signals passed on?
How confidently do the followers move—are they tense or relaxed?

Age group: all ages

Size of group: 6–20

The group divides into pairs. One partner stands entirely relaxed, with eyes closed, while the other arranges her or him in a certain posture. Neither may speak during the game. They then exchange roles.

Variation:

Players use only words to explain how their partners should stand.

What to watch out for:

How do the "sculptors" handle their "statues"—hesitantly, carefully, nervously, self-consciously, gently, or roughly?
Is the "sculptor" able to make his intentions clear to the "statue"?
Is the "statue" able to understand the "sculptor's" intentions?

Discussion aids:

What difficulties arise when only one form of communication is used?

Identification and Empathy
Pyramid

Age group: all ages

Size of group: 8–20

Player B arranges Player A as part of a human pyramid. Player C
then adds Player B to the pyramid, the next player arranges C,
and so on. The last player arranges her- or himself in the design.
No part of the pyramid may stand in isolation from the rest. No
one may speak during the game.

What to watch out for:

What kind of positions are players arranged in—comfortable or
complicated?
Who arranges whom?
Is the pyramid constructed so that players touch one another?

Discussion aids:

What difficulties arise when only nonverbal communication is
used?

Age group: teenagers and adults

Size of group: 8–20

Materials: paper and pens; pieces of paper with various
                  "scenes of action" written on them; pieces of
                  paper with opposite attitudes or types of be-
                  havior on them

Pairs of players who choose to "perform" draw from one pile a
piece of paper with a scene of action on it, such as a courtroom,
filling station, or an executive's office. From another pile they draw
a piece of paper giving opposite attitudes, such as timid/bold,
taciturn/talkative, happy/sad, calm/effervescent. The two players
then devise a skit which corresponds to the instructions picked,
and perform it in front of the group. The audience has to guess
where the scene is set and what kinds of behavior are being
portrayed.

What to watch out for:

How do the performers tackle their task?
What difficulties does the group have in recognizing what is being
portrayed?

7 Identification and Empathy
Famous strangers

Age group: teenagers and adults

Size of group: 8–20

Two players stand facing one another. Each pretends to be a famous person, without telling anyone who they are. The two have to find out who the other is by asking questions alternately. The questions must be asked in such a way that they can be answered "Yes" or "No."

Variation:

The game leader tells the players their partners' "names," but not their own. Using the same method of questioning as above, they have to discover their own identities.

What to watch out for:

What questioning techniques do players use?
Do partners try to help each other or deliberately mislead each other; do they cooperate or compete with each other?

Age group: teenagers and adults

Size of group: 8–20

Materials: depending on the size of the group, 10–15 magazine photos that show people communicating with one another

The game leader shows the group a number of photos of people communicating in any way. Players divide into pairs and each pair chooses a photo, without the others seeing it.

Each couple now performs a conversation that the people in their photo might be having. The other players have to guess which photo they are performing.

What to watch out for:

Does the audience have difficulty in guessing which photo it is? Why?

9 Identification and Empathy
Interrupted scene

Age group: teenagers and adults

Size of group: 8–20

Each of three players (A, B, and C) devises a scene to perform, such as "Sunday morning before church," "car repair shop," "government reception." None of them knows what the others' scenes are.

The game leader arranges a different starting signal with each of them, unknown to the others. When the leader gives A the agreed-upon signal, she or he has to start performing her or his scene. B and C have to try to join in. After a time B is given a signal and she or he must begin the new scene. This time A and C have to try to join in, until C's signal is given. The game may be played verbally or nonverbally.

Age group: teenagers and adults

Size of group: 6–20

This is a role-playing game involving three people: "Father," "Mother," and a "counselor," who asks the parents questions about their roles, their behavior, and their feelings.

At a signal from the game leader players exchange roles: the counselor becomes the mother, the mother becomes the father, and the father becomes the counselor. Later the roles are changed once more so that everyone has played each role once.

Warning:

This game should only be played with groups who are accustomed to games, since the players are given little indication of what to do. Otherwise it may arouse too much anxiety.

11 Identification and Empathy
Guidance officer

Duration:	about 2 hours
Age group:	teenagers and adults
Size of group:	3–18—small groups of three players each or one group in which 3 players perform and the others listen
Materials:	instructions for the mother and the guidance officer

Three people take part in this game: the mother, the guidance officer, and an observer. The mother goes to the guidance officer because her fifteen-year-old daughter has been picked up by the police with a street gang that was causing a disturbance. The girl has several previous convictions and one more will mean she will be sent to a reformatory. The mother has a job and can't look after the daughter properly. She doesn't know what to do to prevent the girl being sent to the reformatory. But the mother has another, and more important reason for going to see the guidance officer: she is divorced and lives with a man, and she has just discovered him in bed with her daughter. She is so upset about this that she will talk about it only if the guidance officer wins her confidence. (Only the person playing the mother and the game leader know beforehand the true reason for the mother's visit.)

Instructions for the "mother" are: "Try to project yourself totally into the role of the mother. Don't mention the true reason for your visit unless the guidance officer really gains your confidence."

Instructions for the "guidance officer" are: "Try to project yourself totally into the role of the guidance officer. The people who come to you are strangers and you can help them only if they tell you their problems frankly and honestly. Remember that many people can only approach their problems indirectly. You personally have nothing to lose in this conversation, but for the mother it may be of immense significance."

What to watch out for:

How does the guidance officer behave—does he give the mother advice, does he discover the truth, does he let the mother find her own solutions, does he only offer his personal opinion, does he judge her, blame her, or tell her what to do?

12 Identification and Empathy
Liberation from sex roles

Duration: about 2 hours

Age group: teenagers and adults

Size of group: 10–20

Materials: paper and pens

Learning goal: players become aware of their prejudices regarding the other sex, and how prejudices unconsciously limit their own behavior

Players divide into two groups, female and male. For about twenty minutes each group discusses the qualities of the opposite sex:
—What is typically masculine?
—What is typically feminine?
Each group chooses a secretary to record its conclusions, and a spokesperson.

Afterward two female and two male players are chosen to perform a role-game, the women playing male roles and the men playing female ones. The purpose of the game should be discussed at this point, but not its development.

The spokespeople report the outcome of group discussions to the group as a whole.

Small (mixed) groups discuss the causes and forms of sex role prejudice.

What to watch out for:

What qualities are considered sex-specific?
Do peoples' attitudes correspond with their own behavior?
Is it possible to avoid sexual roles?
Do the women play normal masculine roles in the role game, and vice versa? Do they exaggerate the "typical" behavior of the opposite sex, or do they develop new forms of behavior?

Discussion aids:

Players should not only liberate themselves from sexual prejudices, they should also come to understand how prejudices arise and what their function is.

Warning:

This game may cause insecurity and anxiety if the behavior of individual players is assessed too closely, and players realize that their behavior is not "ideal."

13 Identification and Empathy
Clubs

Duration:	1 hour
Age group:	teenagers and adults
Size of group:	10–20

Four players leave the room and decide on a club, association, or organization that they will pretend to portray, such as a kennel club, a political party, an employers' association. They choose a chairperson.

They then come back into the room and act out a meeting of the club. They read minutes, put forward proposals, debate them, and make decisions—but all in a veiled way, without directly revealing the type of organization being portrayed. The rest of the group have to guess what kind of club it is. When someone thinks he has guessed, he joins in with the meeting.

What to watch out for:

Is it difficult or easy to detach meaningful statements deliberately from their context? Why?
How clear-cut is this detachment in the game?
How difficult or easy is it for the other players to join in?

Discussion aids:

Players should come to realize that one reason why it is difficult to detach meaningful statements from their context deliberately in a game is that people so often do it subconsciously in everyday conversation.

Age group: teenagers and adults

Size of group: 6–20

Learning goal: to feel your way into roles and imitate the appropriate characteristics of those roles

One player has to make a speech without words on a subject chosen by the group. During the speech she or he has to imitate the gestures of a person known to the group (such as another group member, the game leader, a politician). The other players may also communicate only by gesture.

Warning:

This game should only be played with groups who are accustomed to game-playing.

15 Identification and Empathy
Exchanging roles

Age group: all ages

Size of group: 6–16

Materials: paper and pens

In a group where the players know each other quite well, everyone writes her or his name on a piece of paper. The slips of paper are collected, mixed up, and each player draws one with the name of another member of the group on it.

Everyone then has to say something about this other player, but speaking in the first person, in other words:

—"I am . . ."

—"I often say . . ."

—"I always like . . ."

The statements may be about any characteristic of the other player. The group has to guess who the other person is.

Age group: teenagers and adults

Size of group: 6–20

Two players, A and B, have a discussion. Behind each of them stands a "shadow," A and B. A says or asks something. Then A says what she or he believes A really meant to say, felt, or omitted to say. B answers A and then B interprets what B said. A answers B and so on.

What to watch out for:

Do the shadows really understand what their partners are thinking, feeling, and not saying?
Do the shadows project their own feelings and thoughts onto their partners?
Who steers the conversation, A and B or their shadows?

Age group: all ages

Size of group: 6–14

Learning goal: to put yourself in another person's position, and to hold a conversation for a certain period of time with someone you didn't choose to speak to, on a subject you didn't choose

Players sit in a circle with their eyes closed. The game leader, the "operator," dials a number on an imaginary telephone and "calls" one of the players by tapping her or him on the shoulder. The operator gives this player a name, and connects her or him to another player with an imaginary telephone, who is also assigned a role. The operator then tells the two players what to talk about. They have to imagine that they are a long way apart and the telephone is their only means of communication. At the end of the conversation the operator terminates the connection.

Examples of conversations might be:

—Sally Richardson in New York calls Tom Dunne in Boston to make a date.

—Mrs. Miller calls her friend to complain to her about her husband.

—Mr. Peterson in San Francisco calls his mother in Nashville to congratulate her on her seventieth birthday.

Discussion aids:

What happens in this game depends largely on the game leader, her ideas, and her insight. She can set up conversations between players who rarely speak to one another or who only talk about their own problems.

Age group: all ages

Size of group: 6–20

Learning goal: to interpret and react appropriately to intonation, intensity, melody, pitch, and mood in language, independent of verbal meaning

Gibberish is a language in which people of any nationality can converse and understand each other, even if they only know their own language. The game leader assigns two players a nationality and a situation: for instance, an Englishman and an Eskimo who haven't seen each other for ten years meet on Broadway. The two players try to communicate with one another in a nonsense language.

Warning:

This game is unsuitable for groups who are not accustomed to game-playing or who are inhibited.

19 Identification and Empathy
Taking a trip

Age group: all ages

Size of group: 8–20

Materials: paper and pens

One player, who is "taking a trip," leaves the room. The others pack an imaginary suitcase for her or him, with objects or qualities that the "traveller" possesses or that they would like her or him to have, such as a healthy appetite, last summer's torrential rains, a can of cynicism, a snow-white handkerchief, composure, the ability to cook, tight pants. A list is drawn up, with one contribution from each player, and the traveller is brought back into the room. The list is read to the traveller and she or he has to guess who has packed which object or quality.

Discussion aids:

The game should reveal not only how other group members see the individual, but also how she or he *thinks* they see her or him.

Age group: teenagers and adults

Size of group: 6–10

Materials: paper and pens

Every player draws a card with the name of another group member on it, for whom she or he then has to compose an appropriate "personal" ad. The ads are collected and mixed up, and read aloud one after the other. The group has to guess who wrote them, and on whose behalf.

Variation:

Everyone writes her or his own ad. The group then has to guess who the advertisers are.

21 Identification and Empathy
What would you do if?

Age group: teenagers and adults

Size of group: 6–14

Materials: paper and pens

The game leader asks a series of questions to which players have to write down their answers in rapid succession. The pieces of paper are left unsigned, collected, and read aloud by the game leader. The group has to guess who wrote each one.
Examples might be:
—What would you do if you won a million dollars?
—What's your favorite season?
—What's your favorite food?
—What qualities do you value most in your partner?
—What would you do if your alarm clock went off an hour early?
—Which century would you most like to have lived in?
—What famous person do you admire most?
—Which book would you take to a desert island with you?
—Which country would you most like to visit?
—Which color do you dislike most?
—Which animal do you find most disgusting?
—What do you wish for your friends?
—Would you rather live in the past or in the future?

Age group: teenagers and adults

Size of group: 6–14

Materials: paper and pens

A king (or queen) and a minister are chosen by lot. The king sits on a throne with his minister beside him; the rest of the players stand at the other end of the room. The minister goes over to them and asks each one in turn what she or he objects to about the king. One may dislike the king's appearance, another may be critical of his regime. The minister goes back to the king, tells him all the complaints, and finds out which one annoys the king most. The king then has three chances to guess which of his subjects made this complaint. If he fails to guess correctly the minister has to collect a whole new series of complaints, and the king guesses again.

What to watch out for:

What kind of complaints are made against the king—superficial, banal, things he can't change or behavior that can be changed? Does the king admit what really affects him or does he choose an inoffensive complaint?

23 Identification and Empathy Analogies

Age group: teenagers and adults

Size of group: 6–14

Players try to get to know each other better with the help of analogies. One player in the group thinks of another player, and the rest have to try to find out who it is by asking questions such as:

—What would this person be if she or he were a color?

—What would this person be if she or he were a landscape?

—What would this person be if she or he were a musical instrument?

—What would this person be if . . .?

Age group: teenagers and adults

Size of group: 6–10

Materials: paper and pens

One player chooses an object in the room, tells the rest of the group what it is, and goes out. The other players try to think of qualities that this object and the player who chose it share. They write down the qualities together with the name of the person who chose the object.

The first player is brought back into the room and has to explain to the group why she or he chose this particular object. Then the list of qualities is read out, and she or he has to guess who suggested which ones.

Afterward the first player correctly guessed chooses an object.

Age group: teenagers and adults

Size of group: 6–20

Materials: paper and pens

Each player draws a picture of herself or himself as an animal, to symbolize her or his position in the group. The papers are left unsigned, collected, and then displayed one after another. The group has to guess who drew which animal.

Variation:

Each player is given a card with the name of another group member on it. She or he has to invent a name and animal appropriate to the other person, such as Otto the Tunafish. These are written down on pieces of paper, collected, and read aloud. The players say what qualities they associate with each name and kind of animal; then the writer gives her or his associations, and finally the name of the person she or he was thinking of.

Age group: teenagers and adults

Size of group: 8–20

Players form two groups. Two rows of chairs are arranged facing one another. Group A sits on one row of chairs, and Group B stands behind the other row of chairs, facing Group A. Each of the players sitting down mentally chooses one of the standing players. Each standing player then sits down opposite the player who she or he thinks has chosen her or him. If the player chooses the correct place she or he remains seated and her or his partner has to stand up. If the player chooses the wrong place, she or he has to guess again.

Discussion aids:

The game leader should not take part, so that he can analyze the proceedings without any personal or emotional involvement.

V. Aggression and Self-Assertion

Aggression and Self-Assertion

The word *aggression* derives from *ad-gredi* = approach someone or something. Without going into the various theories of aggression, it is possible to distinguish between two forms. Destructive aggression, which is characteristically irrational and usually expressed in the form of internal or external damage or destruction, has lost its object and can no longer be controlled by the ego. Constructive aggression, on the other hand, enables you to articulate and realize your own needs in relation to an object. This is the form of aggression we are referring to when the word is used in this chapter.

By self-assertion we mean the will and ability to represent your own interests—which may sometimes conflict with the interests of others—and find suitable ways of realizing them.

The games in this section are deliberately conflict-oriented, in other words they aim to make group members aware of conflicts in the group and in society, to question existing behavior patterns and mechanisms for resolving conflict, and to suggest new forms of behavior that can be tried out first in game form.

Your sense of identity and self-respect result from your ability to articulate and assert your own needs and interests. Many people are not capable of doing this, since our society generally condemns the assertion of individual desires. This is a particularly clear example of how personality depends on acquired standards and forms of behavior that have then become internalized. However, the ability to encounter an object, either a person or a thing, constructively knowing your own wishes and needs, is absolutely essential for both social and professional activity.

These games offer players the opportunity to get to know or develop various forms of self-assertion in confrontation with other group members, such as teaming up with like-minded people in order to achieve something more easily. Players can admit, express, and jointly investigate the causes behind feelings of aversion and hatred toward things, methods, or other group members.

Having acquired these abilities, group members will be able

either to eliminate negative feelings, to live with them, or to turn them into a positive force. In addition players become aware of the pressure that exists within the group and the constraints it puts on each of them. They learn to resist certain constraints and, for instance, not to take part in certain games. They also learn to assert their own needs and interests, and allow them to be examined by the group for legitimacy and practicality.

Dangers, limits, practical tips: For these games to be effective it is essential that players understand the importance of learning to assert their own needs. It may be difficult to convince some of them, especially if they read the saying "Love thy neighbor as thyself" with the emphasis on the first part. They must realize that their neighbor's personality is also made up of selfish interests and needs, and that they should not accept and tolerate him more than themselves. Only when we are able to realize our own needs and interests can we help others to recognize and achieve theirs. Unless our self-love and neighborly love are equally balanced, we may lose our sense of identity and no longer even be capable of social charity.

If negative feelings emerge in the group the game leader should not necessarily relieve the tension at once, since tension—used constructively—may stimulate change and solution of problems. If tension is removed too soon and a harmonized but not harmonious group situation created, this stimulation will be lost and players will miss the chance to assert their own desires against opposition for a period of time.

1 Aggression and Self-Assertion
Bridge party

Duration: about 1½ hours

Age group: teenagers and adults

Size of group: 8–20

A group of men friends who haven't seen each other for a long time arranges a bridge party. One of their wives arrives during the evening and tries to get her husband to come home.

Afterward the game is repeated with a group of women friends who haven't seen each other for a long time. A husband attempts to get his wife to come home.

Similarities and differences in behavior will become clear when the two games are compared.

Possible extension: The couple at breakfast next morning.

What to watch out for:

How do people try to convince their partners to leave the party—by argument, cunning, force, or persuasion? Do they threaten sanctions or coldness?
How do the partners resolve the conflict?
How do the friends react?

Discussion aids:

Sexually determined behavior should become clear.

Warning:

It is not advisable for couples who are really married to play this game, since behavior patterns from their own marriage may appear which they may be too upset to deal with.

Age group: teenagers and adults

Size of group: 6–20

Players take turns portraying one of the following situations:

—A customer in a restaurant complains about the food.

—A truck driver on a long haul comes into a bar where there's at least one other customer and a bartender. He wants some cigarettes out of the cigarette machine, but it's out of order and he loses his money. He asks the bartender for his money back, but the bartender claims he's not responsible since the machine belongs to the cigarette company.

—A customer complains to an optician about his new glasses.

—An employee comes to the personnel department to ask for a raise.

—A customer complains to a hairdresser that her or his hair has been cut badly.

—A black student tries to rent a room in a white neighborhood.

—A door-to-door salesman tries to sell a vacuum cleaner.

—At ten minutes to six, two Jehovah's Witnesses try to persuade a man who is determined to watch the evening news on TV to come to one of their meetings.

—A train conductor discovers a passenger whose pass has expired.

—A customer in a shoe store tries to exchange a pair of shoes bought a few days earlier.

—A roomer in a private house is accused of having broken one of the house rules.

—A roomer in a rooming house is accused of having caused a disturbance during the night.

—An uninvited guest tries to get to talk to the "star" at a party of celebrities.

—A daughter tells her mother that she wants to marry a foreigner.

—A father shouts at his daughter for coming home late.

—A son asks his parents for pocket money.

—A son asks his parents if he can stay out later.

—A daughter tries to persuade her parents to let her watch a late movie on television.

—A mother asks her son to do some shopping for her. The son says he doesn't want to. The father comes in and overhears the son's answer.

—Parents catch their daughter smoking hash.

—A gang of teenage girls get caught trying to steal something from a local store.

—A high-school student has been away from school for two days and refuses to take a weekly test. The teacher says the student should know the work for the test in any case; but the student is adamant. The teacher gets furious and takes the student to the principal.

—A girl is tormented by some school friends of her brother's.

—A group of boys torments a smaller group of girls.

—Several people have an argument because they all want to watch different television programs.

—Two drivers have a slight collision. They argue about how it happened. Some witnesses join in.

—A family has an argument because the front door key is lost.

What to watch out for:

How are the conflicts resolved—do some people assert their own interests without considering others? Do some people sacrifice their own interests? Do people compromise?

How do people express their individual needs—objectively, clearly, humorously, or dogmatically, hurtfully, angrily?

Duration: ½ hour–45 minutes

Age group: teenagers and adults

Size of group: several small groups of 6–8 players each

Two groups of equal size sit facing each other. One group plays tourists on a group package vacation visiting a flea market or bazaar. The other group plays local tradespeople who want to sell their wares to the tourists. The game may be played in mime or with words.

What to watch out for:

Do players assume different roles?
Do the tradespeople attempt to sell goods to individuals or to the whole group? Do all the tradespeople descend on one particular tourist?

4 Aggression and Self-Assertion
Scapegoat

Duration:	1 hour
Age group:	all ages
Size of group:	8–20
Learning goal:	to see how a scapegoat mechanism arises and functions

On a camping expedition with some teenagers, the group leader drinks a lot of beer. One day he finds a piece of paper pinned to his tent with the message: "People who drink alcohol all the time shouldn't be youth leaders." He demands to know who wrote it, otherwise he will send everyone home.

The group has to use this synopsis to resolve the conflict in play form.

What to watch out for:

Does the group go along with the leader, are people afraid and anxious to find a scapegoat? Does the group try to find other solutions by talking with the leader?

Discussion aids:

The group should work out possible motives for the leader's behavior, such as fear, insecurity, laziness, or a lust for power.

Age group: teenagers and adults

Size of group: 6–20

Players divide into two groups, "idealists" and "realists." The groups stand facing one another. The idealists make an idealistic statement, to which the realists have to make a realistic reply. Then the realists make a statement and the idealists have to reply, and so on.

Variation:

The game may be played with "optimists" and "pessimists."

What to watch out for:

Do only the quickest and most artful players reply or does everyone contribute? (You could devise a way of giving everyone a turn, such as throwing a ping-pong ball between players in the two groups.)

6 Aggression and Self-Assertion
Eviction

Age group: teenagers and adults

Size of group: 8–16

A group of fellow tenants blocks the entrance to an apartment to prevent the police from evicting a tenant who took part in a rent strike. The police and numerous onlookers tell the demonstrators to obey the law and get out of the way. The police sergeant and a senior police official threaten the tenants with arrest if they continue to block the entrance. Starting from this situation, the group has to resolve the conflict in game form.

What to watch out for:

How are individual interests asserted?
Do the two sides show sympathy for each other?
Do they attempt to persuade each other, or attack or insult each other?

Age group: teenagers and adults

Size of group: 6–14

A cabinet position has become free in a foreign country. There are two candidates. The candidates have to make election speeches in which, instead of praising their own virtues as usual, they have to praise each other's. The one who can demonstrate more convincingly that her or his opponent is the right woman or man for the job wins the election.

What to watch out for:

To what extent do players manage to obey the rules of the game? Are they nevertheless unconsciously ironic or sarcastic?

8 Aggression and Self-Assertion
I want to—no you can't

Duration: 1–1½ hours

Age group: teenagers and adults

Size of group: 8–20

Players divide into several small groups of four to six players each. Each small group then divides into two parties. One party wants to do something and the other forbids it. The "I want to" party should be at least as big, if not bigger, than the other. For twenty minutes the groups devise a role-playing game on this theme and act it out.

The groups then perform their games in front of the rest of the players. Finally the games are discussed in smaller groups.

What to watch out for:

How do groups decide on the subject of the argument?
Do they act out an authority relationship (such as children and parents or teacher) or a relationship between equal partners with opposing interests?
How do they represent their interests—objectively, convincingly, emotionally, persuasively?
How is the prohibition expressed—is it explained, or considered self-evident, absolute?

Age group: teenagers and adults

Size of group: 8–20

Learning goal: how to express aggression, even if indirectly, in a ritualized form

The group sits in a circle. One player starts by making a negative statement and throwing a knotted handkerchief to another member of the group. The other person has to catch the handkerchief and answer, "But I do." She or he then continues in the same way. For example:
—"I don't feel too good today." "But I do."
—"I never drink whisky before lunch." "But I do."
—"I never stand in front of the mirror." "But I do."

What to watch out for:

What kind of statements are made—banal, superficial, things the "receiver" can't change, or statements about behavior that can be changed?

Age group: all ages

Size of group: 8–20

Players divide into two groups of equal size and stand facing each other with their backs against the walls. At a given signal players in one group try to reach the opposite wall, while members of the other group try to stop them.

Variations:

The "attack" may be made spontaneously; without any specific instructions; arm-in-arm.

What to watch out for:

How do players individually or jointly attempt to reach the wall, or prevent their opponents from reaching it?

Warning:

It is advisable to remove glasses before the game starts, and move any sharp or breakable objects out of the game area.

Age group: all ages

Size of group: 8–16

Learning goal: to become aware of feelings that arise on both sides in a conflict situation

Two players stand facing each other, place the palms of their hands together and clench their fingers. At a given signal they try to push each other backward, away from the spot where they are standing. They may break off the struggle any time they choose.

What to watch out for:

Why is the struggle broken off—exhaustion, satisfaction, sense of inferiority, or resignation?
How does the player who gives up feel?
How does the winner behave?

Warning:

There must be plenty of space for the game. Players should be in good physical condition, since the game is tiring.

12 Aggression and Self-Assertion
Pressure and counter-pressure

Age group: all ages

Size of group: 6–16

Learning goal: to respond to other people's wishes without giving up your own

Players move silently about the room. Everyone chooses a partner, so that eventually two groups of equal size stand facing each other in rows. Partners raise their hands and (without touching one another) exert imaginary pressure and counter-pressure to try to make each other move backward. Afterward the two rows of players exert pressure and counter-pressure on each other as groups.

What to watch out for:

Do players respond to pressure with counter-pressure or with resignation?
Which players feel they have won, and which ones feel they have lost?

Warning:

There must be plenty of room. The game is very tiring.

Age group: teenagers and adults

Size of group: 9–15

The situation is a party with several couples, one guest on her or his own, and many other guests. (The rest of the group can join in if they wish.) The single guest has to find a partner from among the couples, in other words "split" one of the couples.

Possible extension: The "divided" couple drives home together afterward and discusses the party. Or: Conversation next morning.

What to watch out for:

How do players attempt to "trap" a partner?
Is their behavior sexually determined?
How does the abandoned partner react?

Discussion aids:

It's essential that the game be played several times over with people of both sexes taking the leading roles. Modes of behavior that arise during the game should not be seen as individual problems but in relation to the sociocultural background of the participants. This is an opportunity to discuss possessiveness.

Warning:

It's definitely not advisable for married couples to play couples in this game unless a psychotherapist is present, since game-playing can easily become serious.

14 Aggression and Self-Assertion
Balloon game

Age group: teenagers and adults

Size of group: 8–16, plus 4 players as an audience

Four people, possibly famous personalities, are in a balloon. The balloon is overloaded. The travellers can land safely only if one of them jumps out of the balloon first. Each of them has to persuade the others that she or he should not be sacrificed.

What to watch out for:

How do players attempt to convince the others of their own importance—by loud or aggressive speeches, by denouncing the others, by threats, by appealing for sympathy or interest, or persuasion?

Warning:

The players in the balloon should be approximately equally aggressive and eloquent, otherwise the outcome of the game will be clear from the start.

Duration: ½–1 hour

Age group: all ages

Size of group: 6–20

Learning goal: for the individual to make clear and assert her or his interests against a solid group

All players except one link arms and form a tight circle. One player stands in the middle and has to try to get out.

What to watch out for:

How does the player in the center try to get out?
Does she or he use persuasive argument, cunning, or physical force?

Warning:

Take your glasses off first.

Age group: all ages

Size of group: 8–15

The group has to produce a machine. First players choose an inventor who has the idea for the machine, and an engineer and several workers who build the machine according to the inventor's instructions out of the rest of the players.

The machine is then set in motion; the players accompany and punctuate their movements with noises.

One player then destroys the machine.

What to watch out for:

Who chooses to destroy the machine?
How does she or he do it?
How does the group react to the destruction? Do they defend themselves, try to stay together, or allow it to happen passively?

Warning:

Take your glasses off first.

Sources

Antons, Klaus: *Praxis der Gruppendynamik*, p. 131, Hogrefe,
Göttingen:
"Building a Tower I" (Communication & Group Formation
#26)—Model by M. J. Flack. Our form of this game is from P.
Sbandi in the periodical *Gruppenpsychotherapie und*

Gruppendynamik, No. 4/70: "Feedback in Sensitivity-training"
"NASA" (Communication & Group Formation #30)—First
printed in J. W. Pfeiffer and J. E. Jones's *A Handbook of
Structured Experiences for Human Relations Training, Vols. 1
& 2*, University Associates Press, Iowa City, 1970

Dirx, Ruth: *Spiele im Haus*, Guttenberg, Frankfurt:
"Description Game II" (Observation & Perception #5)
"Deaf and Dumb" (Observation & Perception #18)
"Insulting the King" (Identification & Empathy #22)

Gööck: *Das grosse Buch der Spiele*, Bertelsmann, Gütersloh:
"Election speech" (Agression & Self-assertion #7)
"But I do" (Agression & Self-assertion #9)

Heimeran: *Spielbuch für Erwachsene,* Heimeran Verlag, Munich,
1935:
"Silent Sociogram" (Identification & Empathy #26)
"What would you do if?" (Identification & Empathy #21)

Rohrer: *Gesellschaft, Gesellschaftsspiele*, Burckhardthaus Verlag,
Geinhausen and Berlin:
"Mime Chain" (Observation & Perception #17)
"Interrupted scene" (Identification & Empathy #9)
"Eviction" (Agression & Self-assertion #6)

Schwalbacher Spielkartei, Verlag Haus Schwalbach
"Famous strangers" (Identification & Empathy #7)